Practical
Pizzas

p^3

This is a P³ Book
First published in 2003

P³
Queen Street House
4 Queen Street
Bath BA1 1HE, UK

ISBN: 1-40540-937-1

Printed in China

NOTE

Cup measurements in this book are for American cups.
This book also uses imperial and metric measurements. Follow the same units
of measurement throughout; do not mix imperial and metric.
All spoon measurements are level: teaspoons are assumed to be 5 ml, and
tablespoons are assumed to be 15 ml. Unless otherwise stated,
milk is assumed to be whole milk, eggs and individual vegetables such as potatoes
are medium, and pepper is freshly ground black pepper.

The nutritional information provided for each recipe is per serving or per person.
Optional ingredients, variations, or serving suggestions have not been
included in the calculations. The times given for each recipe are an approximate
guide only because the preparation times may differ according to the techniques used by
different people and the cooking times may vary as a result of the type of oven used.

Recipes using raw or very lightly cooked eggs should be
avoided by infants, the elderly, pregnant women, convalescents,
and anyone suffering from an illness.

Contents

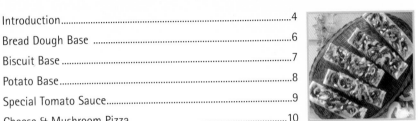

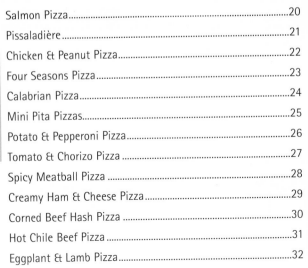

Introduction

Although there is speculation about where pizza in its simplest form was first invented, it is usually associated with the old Italian city of Naples. It was originally a simple street food, richly flavored and quickly made. It was not always round and flat as we know it today, but was originally folded up like a book, with the filling inside, and eaten by hand. Pizzas were usually sold by street criers who carried them around in cylindrical copper drums kept hot with coals from the pizza ovens.

The word "pizza" actually means any kind of pie. The classic Napoletana pizza is probably the best known of the many varieties. It consists of a thin dough crust topped with a fresh tomato sauce, mozzarella cheese, anchovies, olives, and a sprinkling of oregano. When baked, the flavors blend perfectly together to produce the distinctive, aromatic pizza. Another classic is the Margherita, named after an Italian queen. When the queen was on a visit to Naples, she became bored with the usual cuisine and asked to sample a local specialty. The local pizzaiolo created a pizza in the colors of the Italian flag—red tomatoes, green basil, and white mozzarella. The queen was delighted and it became widely celebrated.

As well as being quick to make, economical, and popular, the pizza is more versatile than most other dishes, thanks to the countless possible combinations of bases and toppings that can be served to suit every taste and every occasion.

Fortunately for the busy cook, pizzas are an easy food to chill or freeze, ready to be cooked on demand. There is a wide range of ready-made pizza bases available, as well as dry mixes that only need the addition of water

before they are ready for kneading and baking. You can also make your own. Pizzas are also sold complete with a variety of toppings, which you can bake as they are, or you can add more toppings yourself.

Store-bought pizzas can be very useful to keep at hand. Jars of bell peppers, sun-dried tomatoes, and artichokes in olive oil make very good toppings, and will keep for quite a while in your pantry.

The dough base

Although making your own pizza base can be a little time consuming, the method is straightforward (see recipes on pages 6–8) and you end up with a delicious home-baked dish as well as a sense of achievement. The ingredients are very basic. There are three types of yeast available: fresh, dry, and rapid-rise. Fresh

yeast is usually found in health food stores and is inexpensive. Buy it in bulk and freeze in ½-oz/15-g quantities, ready to use whenever needed. To use, mix ½ oz/15 g fresh yeast in 6 tablespoons of tepid water with ½ teaspoon of sugar, and let dissolve before adding to the flour. This takes about 5 minutes. The frothiness indicates that the yeast is working. Fresh yeast will keep for 4–5 days in the refrigerator. Make sure that it is well covered because it will dry out very quickly.

Dry yeast is sold in packages or small tubs. It has a shelf life of about 6 months, so buy only a small amount if you are not going to make bread dough on a regular basis. Like fresh yeast, add it to the tepid water with a little sugar and stir to dissolve. Let stand for about 10–15 minutes, until froth develops on the surface.

Rapid-rise dry yeast is the simplest form of yeast to use because it is stirred dry into the flour before the water is added. It is sold in packages, which can be found in most stores.

Traditional pizza bases are normally made from bread dough, which is usually made from strong flour. You can also use one of the many types of whole-wheat flours available, such as stoneground, wheatmeal, and granary. Try adding a handful of wheat germ or bran to white flour for extra flavor, fiber, and interest. You could also mix equal quantities of white and whole-wheat flour. Always sift the flour first because this will remove any lumps and help to incorporate air into the flour, which will in turn help to produce a light dough. If you sift whole-wheat flours, there will be some bran and other bits left in the strainer, which are normally then tipped into the mixing bowl so that their goodness and fiber are added to the sifted flour.

Yeast thrives in warm surroundings, so you should make sure that all the ingredients and equipment for the dough are warm before you start. If you add tepid yeast liquid to a cold bowl of cold flour, it will quickly cool down. This will retard the growth of the yeast and the dough will take much longer to rise. So if you keep your flour in a cool cupboard, remember to remove it in

enough time to let it warm to room temperature before you use it. For the best results, sift the flour into a large mixing bowl and then place it somewhere warm, such as in an airing cupboard, or in an oven at its lowest setting. Remember not to let it overheat, however, or this will kill the yeast.

Basic tomato sauce

This is a basic topping sauce for pizzas and is quick and easy to make. It will keep well in a screw-top jar in the refrigerator for up to 1 week. Simply spread a generous amount of this tomato sauce over a pizza base, top with your favorite ingredients, then pop it in the oven for a delicious meal in minutes. To ring the changes, you can also use the Special Tomato Sauce on page 9.

Ingredients

1 tbsp olive oil
1 small onion, chopped
1 garlic clove, crushed
7 oz/200 g canned chopped tomatoes
2 tsp tomato paste
½ tsp sugar
½ tsp dried oregano
1 bay leaf
salt and pepper

1 Heat the olive oil in a pan over low heat. Add the onion and garlic and cook gently in the oil for 5 minutes, or until softened but not browned.

2 Add the tomatoes, tomato paste, sugar, oregano, and bay leaf. Season with salt and pepper, then stir well.

3 Bring the sauce to a boil, cover with a lid, and let simmer gently for about 20 minutes, stirring occasionally, until you have a thickish sauce.

4 Remove the bay leaf and adjust the seasoning. Let cool completely before using.

KEY	
	Simplicity level 1–3 (1 easiest, 3 slightly harder)
	Preparation time
	Cooking time

Bread Dough Base

Traditionally, pizza bases are made from bread dough;
this recipe will give you a base similar to an Italian pizza base.

NUTRITIONAL INFORMATION

Calories 182   Sugars 2g
Protein . . . . .5g   Fat 3g
Carbohydrate . . .36g   Saturates 0.5g

🥣 1½ hrs   🕐 0 mins

SERVES 4

I N G R E D I E N T S

½ oz/15 g fresh yeast, or 1 tsp dry or
rapid-rise dry yeast

6 tbsp tepid water

½ tsp sugar

1 tbsp olive oil, plus extra for greasing

1¼ cups all-purpose flour, plus extra
for dusting

1 tsp salt

1 If using fresh yeast, combine it with
the water and sugar in a bowl. If
using dry yeast, sprinkle it over the surface
of the water and whisk in until dissolved.

2 Let the mixture rest in a warm place
for 10–15 minutes, until frothy on the
surface. Stir in the olive oil.

3 Sift the flour and salt into a large
bowl. If using rapid-rise dry yeast,
stir it in at this point. Make a well in
the center and then pour in the yeast
liquid (without the sugar for rapid-rise
dry yeast).

4 Using either floured hands or a
wooden spoon, mix together to form
a dough. Turn out onto a floured counter
and knead for about 5 minutes, or until
smooth and elastic.

5 Place the dough in a large greased
plastic bag and leave in a warm place
for about 1 hour, or until doubled in size.
Airing cupboards are often the best places
for this process, because the temperature
remains constant.

6 Turn out onto a lightly floured counter
and "knock back" by punching the
dough. This releases any air bubbles,
which would make the pizza uneven.
Knead the dough 4 or 5 times. The dough
is now ready to use.

3

4

6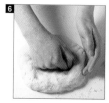

Biscuit Base

This is a quicker alternative to the bread dough base. If you do
not have time to wait for bread dough to rise, a biscuit base is ideal.

NUTRITIONAL INFORMATION

Calories 215   Sugars 3g
Protein . . . . .5g   Fat 7g
Carbohydrate . . .35g   Saturates 4g

 20 mins   🕐 0 mins

SERVES 4

I N G R E D I E N T S

1¼ cups self-rising flour

½ tsp salt

1 oz/25 g butter

½ cup milk

1 Sift the flour and salt into a large mixing bowl.

2 Rub in the butter with your fingertips, until it resembles fine bread crumbs.

3 Make a well in the center of the flour and butter mixture and pour in nearly all of the milk at once. Mix in quickly with a knife. Add the remaining milk only if necessary to mix to a soft dough.

4 Turn the dough out onto a floured counter and knead by turning and pressing with the heel of your hand 3 or 4 times.

5 Either roll out or press the dough into a 10-inch/25-cm circle on a lightly greased cookie sheet or pizza pan. Push up the edge slightly all round to form a ridge and use immediately.

Potato Base

This is an unusual pizza base made from mashed potatoes and flour and is a great way to use up any leftover boiled potatoes.

NUTRITIONAL INFORMATION

Calories 170   Sugars 1g
Protein . . . . .4g   Fat 3g
Carbohydrate . . .34g   Saturates 1g

🥔 2¼ hrs   🕐 0 mins

SERVES 4

I N G R E D I E N T S

8 oz /225 g boiled potatoes

¼ cup butter or margarine

scant 1 cup self-rising flour

½ tsp salt

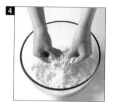

1 If the potatoes are hot, mash them, then stir in the butter until it has melted and is distributed evenly throughout the potatoes. Let cool.

2 Sift the flour and salt together and stir into the cooled mashed potato to form a soft dough.

3 If the potatoes are cold, mash them without adding the butter. Sift the flour and salt into a bowl.

4 Rub in the butter with your fingertips until the mixture resembles fine bread crumbs, then stir the flour and butter mixture into the mashed potatoes to form a soft dough.

5 Either roll out the dough or press it into a 10-inch/25-cm circle on a lightly greased cookie sheet or pizza pan, pushing up the edge slightly all round to form a ridge before adding the topping of your choice. This potato base is somewhat tricky to lift before it is cooked, so you will find it much easier to handle if you roll it out directly onto the cookie sheet, instead of moving it to the cookie sheet after rolling it.

6 If the base is not required for cooking immediately, cover it with plastic wrap and chill it in the refrigerator for up to 2 hours.

Special Tomato Sauce

This sauce is made with fresh tomatoes. Use the plum variety whenever available and always choose the reddest ones for the best flavor.

NUTRITIONAL INFORMATION		
Calories 81	Sugars 6g	
Protein 1g	Fat 6g	
Carbohydrate 6g	Saturates 1g	

🧊 10 mins   🕐 35 mins

SERVES 4

I N G R E D I E N T S

1 small onion, chopped

1 small red bell pepper, chopped

1 garlic clove, crushed

2 tbsp olive oil

8 oz/225 g tomatoes

1 tbsp tomato paste

1 tsp soft brown sugar

2 tsp chopped fresh basil

½ tsp dried oregano

1 bay leaf

salt and pepper

4 Add the tomatoes to the onion mixture with the tomato paste, sugar, basil, oregano, bay leaf, and seasoning. Stir well. Bring to a boil, cover the pan, and simmer gently for about 30 minutes, stirring occasionally, or until you have a thickish sauce.

5 Remove the bay leaf and adjust the seasoning to taste. Let cool completely before using.

6 This sauce will keep well in a screw-top jar in the refrigerator for up to 1 week.

1 Cook the onion, bell pepper, and garlic gently in the oil for 5 minutes, until softened but not browned.

2 Cut a cross in the bottom of each tomato and place them in a bowl. Pour over boiling water and let stand for about 45 seconds. Drain, and then plunge in cold water. The skins will slide off easily.

3 Chop the tomatoes, discarding any hard cores.

Cheese & Mushroom Pizza

This pizza dough is flavored with garlic and herbs and topped with mixed mushrooms and melting cheese for a really delicious pizza.

NUTRITIONAL INFORMATION

Calories . . . . .541 Sugars 5g
Protein . . . . .16g Fat 15g
Carbohydrate . . .91g Saturates 6g

 45 mins   30 mins

SERVES 4

I N G R E D I E N T S

DOUGH

3½ cups strong white flour

2 tsp easy-blend yeast

2 garlic cloves, crushed

2 tbsp chopped fresh thyme

2 tbsp olive oil, plus extra for greasing

1¼ cups tepid water

TOPPING

2 tbsp butter or margarine

12 oz/350 g mixed mushrooms, sliced

2 garlic cloves, crushed

2 tbsp chopped fresh parsley

2 tbsp tomato paste

6 tbsp sieved tomatoes

2¾ oz/75 g mozzarella cheese, grated

salt and pepper

chopped fresh parsley, to garnish

1 Put the flour, yeast, garlic, and thyme in a bowl. Make a well in the center and gradually stir in the oil and water. Bring together to form a soft dough.

2 Turn the dough onto a floured counter and knead for 5 minutes, or until smooth. Roll into a 14-inch/35-cm circle and place on a greased cookie sheet. Let stand in a warm place for 20 minutes, or until the dough puffs up.

3 Meanwhile, make the topping. Melt the butter or margarine in a skillet and sauté the mushrooms, garlic, and parsley for 5 minutes.

4 Mix the tomato paste and sieved tomatoes and spoon onto the pizza base, leaving ½ inch/1 cm of dough around the edge. Spoon the mushroom mixture on top. Season well and sprinkle over the cheese.

5 Cook the pizza in a preheated oven, 375°F/190°C, for 20–25 minutes, or until the bottom is crisp and the cheese has melted. Garnish with chopped parsley and serve.

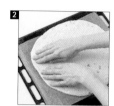

Cheese & Artichoke Pizza

Sliced artichokes combined with sharp colby, Parmesan, and bleu cheese give a really delicious topping to this pizza.

NUTRITIONAL INFORMATION

Calories . . . . . . .424 Sugars 9g
Protein . . . . .16g Fat 20g
Carbohydrate . . .47g Saturates 8g

1¾ hrs   20 mins

SERVES 4

I N G R E D I E N T S

1 quantity Bread Dough Base (see page 6)

1 quantity Special Tomato Sauce (see page 9)

2¼ oz/60 g bleu cheese, sliced

4½ oz/125 g artichoke hearts in oil, sliced

½ small red onion, chopped

1½ oz/40 g sharp colby cheese, grated

2 tbsp freshly grated Parmesan

1 tbsp chopped fresh thyme

oil from artichokes, for drizzling

salt and pepper

TO SERVE

salad greens

cherry tomatoes, halved

1 Roll out or press the dough on a lightly floured counter, using a rolling pin or your hands, to form a 10-inch/25-cm circle.

2 Place the dough circle on a large greased cookie sheet or pizza pan and push up the edge slightly. Cover and let rise for 10 minutes in a warm place.

3 Spread the tomato sauce almost to the edge of the dough circle. Arrange the bleu cheese on top of the tomato sauce, followed by the artichoke hearts and red onion.

4 Mix the colby and Parmesan cheeses together with the thyme and sprinkle the mixture over the pizza. Drizzle a little of the oil from the jar of artichokes over the pizza and season to taste.

5 Bake in a preheated oven, 400°F/200°C, for 18–20 minutes, or until the edge is crisp and golden and the cheese is bubbling.

6 Mix the fresh salad greens and cherry tomato halves together and serve with the pizza, cut into slices.

Red Onion Pizza

The vibrant colors of the bell peppers and red onion make this a delightful pizza. Served cut into fingers, this pizza is ideal for a party or buffet.

NUTRITIONAL INFORMATION

Calories	380	Sugars	........19g
Protein	.........7g	Fat	..........17g
Carbohydrate	...53g	Saturates	.......2g

2½ hrs   25 mins

SERVES 8

I N G R E D I E N T S

1 quantity Bread Dough Base (see page 6)

2 tbsp olive oil

½ each red, green, and yellow bell pepper, thinly sliced

1 small red onion, thinly sliced

1 garlic clove, crushed

1 quantity Basic Tomato Sauce (see page 5)

3 tbsp raisins

1 oz/25 g pine nuts

1 tbsp chopped fresh thyme

2 tbsp olive oil, for greasing and drizzling

salt and pepper

1 Roll out or press the dough, using a rolling pin or your hands, on a lightly floured counter to fit a 12 x 7-inch/ 30 x 18-cm greased jelly roll pan. Place the dough in the pan and push up the edges slightly.

2 Cover and leave the dough to rise slightly in a warm place for about 10 minutes.

3 Heat the oil in a large skillet. Add the sliced bell peppers and red onion, and the crushed garlic, and cook gently for 5 minutes, until they have softened but not browned. Let cool.

4 Spread the tomato sauce over the base of the pizza almost to the edge.

5 Sprinkle over the raisins and top with the cooled bell pepper mixture. Add the pine nuts and thyme. Drizzle with a little olive oil and season well.

6 Bake in a preheated oven, at 400°F/ 200°C, for 18–20 minutes, or until the edges are crisp and golden. Cut into fingers and serve immediately.

Florentine Pizza

A pizza adaptation of Eggs Florentine—sliced hard-cooked eggs on freshly cooked spinach, with a crunchy almond topping.

NUTRITIONAL INFORMATION

Calories ....462 Sugars 6g
Protein ....18g Fat 26g
Carbohydrate ...41g Saturates 8g

3 hrs   20 mins

SERVES 4

I N G R E D I E N T S

2 tbsp freshly grated Parmesan

1 quantity Potato Base dough (see page 8)

1 quantity Basic Tomato Sauce (see page 5)

6 oz/175 g spinach

1 small red onion, thinly sliced

3 tbsp olive oil, plus extra for greasing

¼ tsp freshly grated nutmeg

2 hard-cooked eggs

½ oz/15 g fresh white bread crumbs

2¼ oz/60 g Jarlsberg, grated (or colby or
   Swiss cheese, if not available)

2 tbsp slivered almonds

salt and pepper

1 Mix the Parmesan with the potato base dough. Roll out or press the dough, using a rolling pin or your hands, into a 10-inch/25-cm circle on a lightly floured counter. Place on a large greased cookie sheet or pizza pan and push up the edge slightly. Spread the tomato sauce almost to the edge.

2 Remove the stalks from the spinach and wash the leaves thoroughly in plenty of cold water. Drain well and pat off the excess water with paper towels.

3 Cook the onion gently in 2 tablespoons of the oil for 5 minutes, or until softened. Add the spinach and continue to cook until just wilted. Drain off any excess liquid. Arrange on the pizza and sprinkle over the nutmeg.

4 Shell the eggs, cut into slices, and arrange on top of the spinach.

5 Mix together the bread crumbs, cheese, and almonds, and sprinkle over. Drizzle with the remaining olive oil and season with salt and pepper to taste.

6 Bake in a preheated oven, at 400°F/ 200°C, for 18–20 minutes, or until the edge of the pizza is crisp and golden. Serve immediately.

Giardiniera Pizza

As the name implies, this colorful pizza should be topped with fresh vegetables from the garden, especially in the summer months.

NUTRITIONAL INFORMATION

Calories ....362 Sugars 10g
Protein ....13g Fat 15g
Carbohydrate ...48g Saturates 5g

🥧 3½ hrs   🕐 20 mins

SERVES 4

INGREDIENTS

6 spinach leaves

1 quantity Potato Base (see page 8)

1 quantity Special Tomato Sauce (see page 9)

1 tomato, sliced

1 celery stalk, thinly sliced

½ green bell pepper, thinly sliced

1 baby zucchini, sliced

1 oz/25 g asparagus tips

1 oz/25 g corn, defrosted if frozen

1 oz/25 g peas, defrosted if frozen

4 scallions, trimmed and chopped

1 tbsp chopped fresh mixed herbs

2¼ oz/60 g mozzarella, grated

2 tbsp freshly grated Parmesan

1 artichoke heart

olive oil, for drizzling

salt and pepper

greased cookie sheet or pizza pan and push up the edge a little. Spread with the tomato sauce.

3 Arrange the spinach leaves on the sauce, followed by the tomato slices. Top with the celery, bell pepper, zucchini, asparagus, corn, peas, scallions, and chopped mixed herbs.

4 Mix together the cheeses and sprinkle over the pizza. Place the artichoke heart in the center. Drizzle the pizza with a little olive oil and season.

5 Bake in a preheated oven, 400°F/ 200°C, for 18–20 minutes, or until the edges are crisp and golden brown. Serve immediately.

1 Remove any tough stalks from the spinach and wash the leaves in cold water. Pat dry with paper towels.

2 Roll out or press the potato base on a lightly floured counter, using a rolling pin or your hands, into a large 10-inch/ 25-cm circle. Place the circle on a large

Roasted Vegetable Pizza

For this pizza, beautifully colorful vegetables are roasted in olive oil with thyme and garlic. The goat cheese adds a nutty, piquant flavor.

NUTRITIONAL INFORMATION

Calories 387	Sugars 9g	
Protein 10g	Fat 21g	
Carbohydrate ...42g	Saturates 5g	

2½ hrs   40 mins

SERVES 4

INGREDIENTS

2 baby zucchini, halved lengthwise

2 baby eggplants, cut into fourths lengthwise

½ red bell pepper, cut into 4 strips

½ yellow bell pepper, cut into 4 strips

1 small red onion, cut into wedges

2 garlic cloves, unpeeled

4 tbsp olive oil

1 tbsp red wine vinegar

1 tbsp chopped fresh thyme

1 quantity Bread Dough Base (see page 6)

1 quantity Basic Tomato Sauce (see page 5)

3¼ oz/90 g goat cheese

salt and pepper

fresh basil leaves, to garnish

1 Place the zucchini, eggplants, red and yellow bell peppers, onion, and garlic in a large roasting pan. Mix together the olive oil, vinegar, thyme, and plenty of seasoning and pour over, coating the vegetables well.

2 Roast the vegetables in a preheated oven, 400°F/200°C, for 15–20 minutes, turning half-way through the cooking time, until the skins have started to blacken in places. Let rest for 5 minutes after roasting.

3 Carefully peel off the skins from the roasted bell peppers and the garlic cloves. Slice the garlic.

4 Roll out or press the dough on a lightly floured counter, using a rolling pin or your hands, into a 10-inch/25-cm circle. Place the dough on a large greased cookie sheet or pizza pan and raise the edge a little. Cover and leave in a warm place for 10 minutes to rise slightly. Spread with the tomato sauce almost to the edge of the dough.

5 Arrange the roasted vegetables on top of the sauce and dot with the cheese. Drizzle the oil and juices from the roasting pan over the pizza and adjust the seasoning.

6 Bake in a preheated oven, 400°F/ 200°C, for 18–20 minutes, or until the edge is crisp and golden. Serve immediately, garnished with basil leaves.

Vegetable Calzone

These pizza base parcels are great for making in advance and freezing—they can be defrosted when required for a quick snack.

NUTRITIONAL INFORMATION

Calories 499	Sugars 7g
Protein 16g	Fat 9g
Carbohydrate ...95g	Saturates 2g

1½ hrs   40 mins

SERVES 4

INGREDIENTS

DOUGH

3½ cups strong white flour

2 tsp rapid-rise dry yeast

1 tsp superfine sugar

⅔ cup vegetable bouillon

⅔ cup sieved tomatoes

beaten egg, for glazing

FILLING

1 tbsp vegetable oil, plus extra for greasing

1 onion, chopped

1 garlic clove, crushed

2 tbsp chopped sun-dried tomatoes

3½ oz/100 g spinach, chopped

3 tbsp canned and drained corn

1 oz/25 g green beans, each cut into 3 pieces

1 tbsp tomato paste

1 tbsp chopped oregano

1¾ oz/50 g mozzarella cheese, sliced

salt and pepper

1 Sift the flour into a bowl. Add the yeast and sugar and beat in the vegetable bouillon and sieved tomatoes to make a smooth dough.

2 Knead the dough on a lightly floured counter for 10 minutes, then place in a clean, lightly oiled bowl and leave to rise in a warm place for 1 hour.

3 Heat the oil in a skillet and sauté the onion for 2–3 minutes.

4 Stir in the garlic, tomatoes, spinach, corn, and green beans and cook for 3–4 minutes. Add the tomato paste and oregano, and season with salt and pepper to taste.

5 Divide the risen dough into 4 equal portions and roll each onto a floured counter to form a 7-inch/18-cm circle.

6 Spoon one fourth of the filling onto one half of each circle and top with mozzarella cheese. Fold the dough over to encase the filling, sealing the edge with a fork. Glaze with beaten egg. Put the calzone on a lightly greased cookie sheet and cook in a preheated oven, at 425°F/220°C, for 25–30 minutes, until risen and golden. Serve warm.

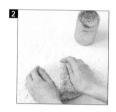

Bean Curd & Corn Pizza

Chunks of bean curd marinated in ginger and soy sauce impart something of an Asian flavor to this pizza.

NUTRITIONAL INFORMATION

Calories 596	Sugars 17g	
Protein 33g	Fat 23g	
Carbohydrate ...66g	Saturates 9g	

1 hr   35 mins

SERVES 4

I N G R E D I E N T S

4¼ cups milk

1 tsp salt

8 oz/225 g semolina

1 tbsp soy sauce

1 tbsp dry sherry

½ tsp grated fresh gingerroot

9 oz/250 g bean curd, cut into chunks

2 eggs

2¼ oz/60 g Parmesan, grated

1 quantity Basic Tomato Sauce (see page 5)

1 oz/25 g baby corn, each cut into 4 pieces

1 oz/25 g snow peas, each trimmed and cut into 4 pieces

4 scallions, each trimmed and cut into 1-inch/2.5-cm strips

2¼ oz/60 g mozzarella, thinly sliced

2 tsp sesame oil, plus extra for greasing

salt and pepper

2 Mix the soy sauce, sherry, and ginger together in a bowl, add the bean curd, and stir gently to coat. Leave to marinate in a cool place for 20 minutes.

3 Beat the eggs with a little pepper. Add the eggs and Parmesan to the semolina and mix well. Place on a large greased cookie sheet or pizza pan and pat into a 10-inch/25-cm circle, using the back of a metal spoon. Spread the tomato sauce almost to the edge.

4 Blanch the corn and snow peas in a pan of boiling water for 1 minute, drain, and place on the pizza with the drained bean curd. Top with the scallions and slices of mozzarella cheese. Drizzle over the sesame oil and season with salt and pepper.

5 Bake in a preheated oven, at 400°F/ 200°C, for 18–20 minutes, or until the edge of the pizza is crisp and golden. Serve immediately.

1 Put the milk and salt in a pan and bring to a boil. Sprinkle the semolina over the surface, stirring all the time. Cook for 10 minutes over low heat, stirring occasionally, taking care not to let it burn. Remove from the heat and let the mixture cool until tepid.

Tomato & Bell Pepper Pizza

This pizza, which is similar to the French Pissaladière, is made with a pastry base flavored with cheese and topped with a delicious sauce.

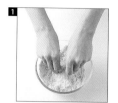

NUTRITIONAL INFORMATION

Calories	611	Sugars	........8g
Protein	.......14g	Fat	.........38g
Carbohydrate	...56g	Saturates	.....21g

  25 mins, plus 30 mins chilling 55 mins

SERVES 4

INGREDIENTS

generous 1½ cups all-purpose flour

4½ oz/125 g butter, diced

½ tsp salt

2 tbsp dried Parmesan cheese

1 egg, beaten

2 tbsp cold water

2 tbsp olive oil

1 large onion, finely chopped

1 garlic clove, chopped

14 oz/400 g canned chopped tomatoes

4 tbsp concentrated tomato paste

1 red bell pepper, halved

5 sprigs of thyme, stalks removed

6 black olives, pitted and halved

1 oz/25 g fresh Parmesan cheese, grated

1 Sift the flour and rub in the butter to make bread crumbs. Stir in the salt and dried Parmesan. Add the egg and 1 tablespoon of the water and mix with a round-bladed knife. Add more water if necessary to make a soft dough. Cover with plastic wrap and chill for 30 minutes.

2 Meanwhile, heat the oil in a skillet and cook the onion and garlic for 5 minutes or until golden. Add the tomatoes and cook for 8–10 minutes. Stir in the tomato paste.

3 Place the bell pepper, skin-side up, on a cookie sheet and cook under a preheated broiler for 15 minutes, until charred. Place in a plastic bag and leave to sweat for 10 minutes. Peel off the skin and slice the flesh into thin strips.

4 Roll out the dough to fit a 9-inch/ 23-cm loose-bottomed fluted tart pan. Line with foil and bake in a preheated oven at 400°F/200°C for 10 minutes, or until just set. Remove the foil and bake for 5 minutes, until lightly golden. Let cool slightly.

5 Spoon the tomato sauce over the pastry base and top with the bell peppers, thyme, olives, and fresh Parmesan. Return to the oven for 15 minutes, or until the pastry is crisp. Serve warm or cold.

Seafood Pizza

Make a change from the standard pizza toppings—this dish is piled high with seafood baked with a red bell pepper and tomato sauce.

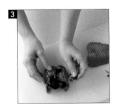

NUTRITIONAL INFORMATION

Calories	248	Sugars	.........7g
Protein	........27g	Fat	...........6g
Carbohydrate	...22g	Saturates	......2g

   25 mins   55 mins

SERVES 4

I N G R E D I E N T S

5 oz/140 g standard pizza base mix

4 tbsp chopped fresh dill or 2 tbsp dried dill

sprigs of fresh dill, to garnish

S A U C E

1 large red bell pepper

14 oz/400 g canned chopped tomatoes with onion and herbs

3 tbsp tomato paste

salt and pepper

T O P P I N G

12 oz/350 g assorted cooked seafood, thawed if frozen

1 tbsp capers in brine, drained

1 oz/25 g pitted black olives in brine, drained

1 oz/25 g lowfat mozzarella cheese, grated

1 tbsp grated fresh Parmesan cheese

1 Preheat the oven to 400°F/200°C. Place the pizza base mix in a bowl and stir in the dill. Make the pizza base dough according to the instructions on the package.

2 Press the dough into a circle measuring 10 inches/25 cm across on a cookie sheet lined with baking parchment. Set aside to rise.

3 Preheat the broiler to hot. To make the sauce, halve and seed the bell pepper and arrange on a broiler rack. Cook for 8–10 minutes, until charred. Cool slightly, peel off the skin, and chop the flesh.

4 Place the tomatoes and bell pepper in a pan. Bring to a boil and simmer for 10 minutes. Stir in the tomato paste and season to taste.

5 Spread the sauce over the pizza base and top with the seafood. Sprinkle over the capers and olives, top with the cheeses, and bake for 25–30 minutes.

6 Garnish with sprigs of fresh dill and serve hot.

Salmon Pizza

You can use either red or pink salmon for this tasty pizza. Red salmon will give a better color and flavor but it can be expensive.

NUTRITIONAL INFORMATION

Calories 321   Sugars 6g
Protein . . . . .12g   Fat 14g
Carbohydrate . . .39g   Saturates 6g

1¼ hrs   20 mins

SERVES 4

INGREDIENTS

1 quantity Biscuit Base (see page 7)

1 quantity Basic Tomato Sauce (see page 5)

1 zucchini, grated

1 tomato, thinly sliced

3½ oz/100 g canned red or pink salmon

2¼ oz/60 g button mushrooms,
   wiped and sliced

1 tbsp chopped fresh dill

½ tsp dried oregano

1½ oz/40 g mozzarella cheese, grated

olive oil, for drizzling

salt and pepper

sprig of fresh dill, to garnish

1 Roll out or press the dough, using a rolling pin or your hands, into a 10-inch/25-cm circle on a lightly floured counter. Place the dough circle on a large greased cookie sheet or pizza pan and push up the edge a little with your fingers to form a rim.

2 Spread the tomato sauce over the pizza base, almost to the edge.

3 Top the tomato sauce with the grated zucchini, then lay the tomato slices on top.

4 Drain the can of salmon. Remove any bones and skin, and flake the fish. Arrange on the pizza with the mushrooms. Sprinkle over the herbs and cheese. Drizzle with a little olive oil and season with salt and pepper.

5 Bake in a preheated oven, at 400°F/200°C, for about 18–20 minutes, or until the edge is golden and crisp.

6 Transfer to a warmed serving plate and serve immediately, garnished with a sprig of dill.

COOK'S TIP

If salmon is too expensive, you can use either canned tuna or sardines instead to make a delicious everyday fish pizza. Choose canned fish in brine for a healthier topping. If fresh dill is unavailable, you can use parsley instead.

Pissaladière

This is a variation of the classic Italian pizza. It originates in Nice and uses ready-made puff pastry, creating a dish perfect for outdoor eating.

NUTRITIONAL INFORMATION

Calories 612   Sugars 13g
Protein . . . . .12g   Fat 43g
Carbohydrate . . .47g   Saturates 11g

20 mins   55 mins

SERVES 8

INGREDIENTS

4 tbsp olive oil, plus extra for greasing

1 lb 9 oz/700 g red onions, thinly sliced

2 garlic cloves, crushed

2 tsp superfine sugar

2 tbsp red wine vinegar

1–2 tbsp flour, for dusting

12 oz/350 g fresh ready-made puff pastry

salt and pepper

TOPPING

3½ oz/100 g canned anchovy fillets

12 green olives, pitted

1 tsp dried marjoram

1 Lightly grease a jelly roll pan. Put the olive oil in a large pan and heat gently. Add the red onions and garlic and cook over low heat for about 30 minutes, stirring occasionally.

2 Add the sugar and red wine vinegar to the pan and season with plenty of salt and pepper.

3 On a lightly floured counter, roll out the pastry to a rectangle, measuring about 13 x 9 inches/33 x 23 cm. Place the pastry rectangle onto the prepared pan, using your fingers to push the pastry into the corners of the pan.

4 Remove the onion mixture from the heat and spread over the pastry.

5 Arrange the anchovy fillets and green olives on top, then sprinkle with the dried marjoram.

6 Bake in a preheated oven, at 425°F/ 220°C, for 20-25 minutes, or until the pissaladière is lightly golden. Serve the pissaladière piping hot, straight from the oven.

VARIATION
Cut the pissaladière into squares or triangles for easy finger food at a party.

Chicken & Peanut Pizza

This pizza is topped with chicken that has been marinated in a delicious peanut sauce.

NUTRITIONAL INFORMATION

Calories . . . . .418 Sugars 7g
Protein . . . . .22g Fat 19g
Carbohydrate . . .43g Saturates 5g

  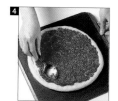 

2¾ hrs   20 mins

SERVES 4

INGREDIENTS

2 tbsp crunchy peanut butter

1 tbsp lime juice

1 tbsp soy sauce

3 tbsp milk

1 red chile, seeded and chopped

1 garlic clove, crushed

6 oz/175 g cooked chicken, diced

1 quantity Bread Dough Base (see page 6)

1 quantity Special Tomato Sauce (see page 9)

4 scallions, trimmed and chopped

2¼ oz/60 g mozzarella cheese, grated

olive oil, for drizzling

salt and pepper

1 Mix together the peanut butter, lime juice, soy sauce, milk, chile, and garlic in a bowl to form a sauce. Season well.

2 Add the chicken to the peanut sauce and stir until well coated. Cover and leave to marinate in a cool place for about 20 minutes.

3 Roll out or press the dough, using a rolling pin or your hands, into a 10-inch/25-cm circle on a lightly floured counter. Place on a large greased cookie sheet or pizza pan and push up the edge a little. Cover and leave to rise slightly for 10 minutes in a warm place.

4 When the dough has risen, spread the tomato sauce over the base, almost to the edge.

5 Top with the chopped scallions and chicken pieces, spooning over the peanut sauce.

6 Sprinkle over the cheese. Drizzle with a little olive oil and season well. Bake in a preheated oven, at 400°F/200°C, for 18–20 minutes, or until the crust is golden. Serve.

Four Seasons Pizza

This is a traditional pizza on which the toppings are divided into four sections, each of which is supposed to depict a season of the year.

NUTRITIONAL INFORMATION

Calories . . . . .313 Sugars 8g
Protein . . . . .8g Fat 13g
Carbohydrate . . .44g Saturates 3g

2¾ hrs   20 mins

SERVES 4

INGREDIENTS

1 quantity Bread Dough Base (see page 6)

1 tbsp flour, for dusting

1 quantity Special Tomato Sauce (see page 9)

1 oz/25 g chorizo sausage, thinly sliced

1 oz/25 g button mushrooms, wiped and thinly sliced

1½ oz/40 g artichoke hearts, thinly sliced

1 oz/25 g mozzarella, thinly sliced

3 anchovies, halved lengthwise

2 tsp capers

4 black olives, pitted and sliced

4 fresh basil leaves, shredded

olive oil, for greasing and drizzling

salt and pepper

1 Roll out or press the dough, using a rolling pin or your hands, into a 10-inch/25-cm circle on a lightly floured counter. Place on a large greased cookie sheet or pizza pan and push up the edge a little.

2 Cover and let rise for 10 minutes in a warm place. Spread the tomato sauce over the pizza base, almost to the edge.

3 Put the sliced chorizo onto one fourth of the pizza, the sliced mushrooms on another fourth, the artichoke hearts on another fourth, and the mozzarella and anchovies on the last.

4 Dot with the capers, olives, and basil. Drizzle with a little olive oil and season, but do not put any salt on the anchovy section because the fish are very salty.

5 Bake in a preheated oven, at 400°F/ 200°C, for 18–20 minutes, or until the crust is golden and crisp. Serve the pizza immediately.

Calabrian Pizza

Traditionally, this pizza has a double layer of dough to make it robust and filling. Alternatively, it can be made as a single pizza (as shown here).

NUTRITIONAL INFORMATION

Calories ......574 Sugars 6g
Protein ....20g Fat 30g
Carbohydrate ...60g Saturates 7g

🍲 2½ hrs   🕐 55 mins

SERVES 6

INGREDIENTS

DOUGH

generous 3 cups all-purpose flour, plus extra for dusting

½ tsp salt

1 package rapid-rise dry yeast

2 tbsp olive oil, plus extra for greasing

about generous 1 cup warm water

FILLING

2 tbsp olive oil

2 garlic cloves, crushed

1 red bell pepper, cored, seeded, and sliced

1 yellow bell pepper, cored, seeded, and sliced

4½ oz/125 g ricotta cheese

6 oz/175 g jar sun-dried tomatoes, drained

3 hard-cooked eggs, thinly sliced

1 tbsp chopped fresh mixed herbs

4½ oz/125 g salami, cut into strips

5½–6 oz/150–175 g mozzarella, grated

a little milk, to glaze

salt and pepper

1 Sift the flour and salt into a bowl and mix in the rapid-rise dry yeast.

2 Add the olive oil and enough warm water to mix to a smooth, pliable dough. Knead for 10–15 minutes by hand, or process for 5 minutes in a mixer.

3 Shape the dough into a ball, place in a lightly oiled plastic bag, and put in a warm place for 1–1½ hours, or until doubled in size.

4 To make the filling, heat the oil in a skillet and cook the garlic and bell peppers slowly in the oil, until softened.

5 Knock back the dough on a lightly floured counter and then roll out half of it to fit the bottom of a 12 x 10-inch/ 30 x 25-cm oiled roasting pan.

6 Season the dough and spread with the ricotta cheese, then cover with sun-dried tomatoes, hard-cooked eggs, herbs, and the bell pepper mixture. Arrange the salami strips on top and sprinkle with the grated mozzarella.

7 Roll out the remaining dough and place over the filling, sealing the edges well, or use to make a second pizza. Leave to rise for 1 hour in a warm place. An uncovered pizza will take only about 30–40 minutes to rise.

8 Prick the double pizza with a fork about 20 times, brush the top with milk, and cook in a preheated oven, at 350°F/180°C, for about 50 minutes, or until lightly browned. The uncovered pizza will take only 35–40 minutes to cook. Serve hot.

 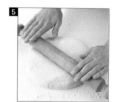 

Mini Pita Pizzas

Smoked salmon and asparagus make extra-special party pizza canapés.
Mini pitas make great bases and are really quick to cook.

NUTRITIONAL INFORMATION

Calories 518   Sugars 10g
Protein . . . . .21g   Fat 12g
Carbohydrate . . .87g   Saturates 4g

 55 mins   15 mins

SERVES 4

I N G R E D I E N T S

8 thin asparagus spears

16 mini pitas

1 quantity Special Tomato Sauce (see page 9)

1 oz/25 g mild colby cheese, grated

1 oz/25 g ricotta cheese

2¼ oz/60 g smoked salmon

olive oil, for drizzling

pepper

1 Cut the asparagus spears into 1-inch/
2.5-cm lengths, then cut each piece
in half lengthwise.

2 Blanch the asparagus in a pan of
boiling water for 1 minute. Drain the
asparagus, plunge into cold water, and
drain again.

3 Place the pitas on 2 cookie sheets.
Spread about 1 teaspoon of tomato
sauce on each pita.

4 Mix the colby cheese and ricotta
cheese together and divide between
the 16 pitas.

5 Cut the smoked salmon into 16 long,
thin strips. Arrange one strip on each
pita and add the asparagus spears.

6 Drizzle over a little olive oil and
season with pepper to taste.

7 Bake the pizzas in a preheated oven,
at 400°F/200°C, for 8–10 minutes.
Serve immediately.

COOK'S TIP

Smoked salmon is expensive,
so for a cheaper version, use
smoked trout. It is often half the
price of smoked salmon, and tastes
just as good. Try experimenting with
other smoked fish, such as smoked
mackerel, with its strong, distinctive
flavor, for a bit of variety.

Potato & Pepperoni Pizza

Potatoes make a great pizza base and this recipe is well worth making, both for texture and flavor.

NUTRITIONAL INFORMATION

Calories 234   Sugars 5g
Protein . . . . .4g   Fat 12g
Carbohydrate . . .30g   Saturates 1g

  20 mins   🕐 45 mins

SERVES 4

INGREDIENTS

1 tbsp butter, plus extra for greasing

flour, for dusting

2 lb/900 g mealy potatoes, diced

2 garlic cloves, crushed

2 tbsp chopped fresh mixed herbs

1 egg, beaten

⅓ cup sieved tomatoes

2 tbsp tomato paste

1¾ oz/50 g pepperoni slices

1 green bell pepper, cut into strips

1 yellow bell pepper, cut into strips

2 large open-cap mushrooms, sliced

1 oz/25 g pitted black olives, cut into fourths

4½ oz/125 g mozzarella cheese, sliced

1 Grease and flour a 9-inch/23-cm pizza pan.

2 Cook the diced potatoes in a pan of boiling water for 10 minutes, or until cooked through. Drain and mash, until smooth. Transfer the mashed potato to a mixing bowl and stir in the remaining butter, and the garlic, herbs, and egg.

3 Spread the mixture into the prepared pizza pan. Cook in a preheated oven, 425°F/220°C, for 7–10 minutes, or until the pizza base begins to set.

4 Mix the sieved tomatoes and tomato paste together and spoon over the pizza base, to within ½ inch/1 cm of the edge of the base.

5 Arrange the pepperoni, green and yellow bell peppers, mushrooms, and olives on top of the sieved tomatoes.

6 Arrange the mozzarella cheese on top of the pizza. Return to the oven for 20 minutes, or until the bottom is cooked through and the cheese has melted on top. Serve hot.

COOK'S TIP

This pizza base is softer in texture than a normal bread dough and is ideal served from the pan. Top with any of your favorite pizza ingredients that you have at hand.

Tomato & Chorizo Pizza

Spicy chorizo sausage blends beautifully with juicy tomatoes and melting mozzarella cheese in this recipe. This pizza makes a delicious light lunch.

NUTRITIONAL INFORMATION

Calories 574   Sugars 8g
Protein ....17g   Fat 38g
Carbohydrate ...43g   Saturates 8g

 15 mins   🕐 15 mins

SERVES 2

I N G R E D I E N T S

9-inch/23-cm ready-made pizza base

1 tbsp black olive paste

1 tbsp olive oil

1 onion, sliced

1 garlic clove, crushed

4 tomatoes, sliced

3 oz/85 g chorizo sausage, sliced

1 tsp fresh oregano

4½ oz/125 g mozzarella cheese, sliced

6 black olives, pitted and halved

pepper

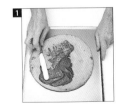
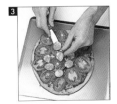

1 Put the pizza base on a cookie sheet and spread the black olive paste to within ½ inch/1 cm of the edge.

2 Heat the oil in a skillet and cook the onion for 2 minutes. Add the garlic and cook for 1 minute.

3 Spread the onion mixture over the pizza base and arrange the tomatoes and chorizo slices on top. Sprinkle with the oregano, season with pepper to taste, and arrange the mozzarella cheese and olives on top.

4 Bake in a preheated oven, 450°F/230°C/, for 10 minutes, until the cheese is melted and golden. Serve the pizza immediately.

COOK'S TIP

There are several varieties of pizza base available. Those with added olive oil are preferable because the dough is much lighter and tastier.

Spicy Meatball Pizza

Small ground beef meatballs, spiced with chiles and cumin seeds, are baked on a biscuit base in this recipe.

NUTRITIONAL INFORMATION

Calories ....568 Sugars 5g
Protein ....24g Fat 37g
Carbohydrate ...38g Saturates 15g

2¼ hrs   25 mins

SERVES 4

INGREDIENTS

8 oz/225 g ground lean beef

1 oz/25 g jalapeño chiles in brine, chopped

1 tsp cumin seeds

1 tbsp chopped fresh parsley

1 tbsp beaten egg

3 tbsp olive oil, plus extra for greasing

1 quantity Biscuit Base dough (see page 7)

1 quantity Basic Tomato Sauce (see page 5)

1 oz/25 g canned pimientos, sliced

2 slices streaky bacon, cut into strips

2¼ oz/60 g sharp colby cheese, grated

olive oil, for drizzling

salt and pepper

chopped fresh parsley, to garnish

1 Mix the beef, chiles, cumin seeds, parsley, and egg together in a bowl and season. Form into 12 small meatballs. Cover and chill for 1 hour.

2 Heat the oil in a large skillet. Add the meatballs and brown all over. Remove with a perforated spoon or fish slice and drain on paper towels.

3 Roll out or press the dough into a 10-inch/25-cm circle on a lightly floured counter. Place on a greased cookie sheet or pizza pan and push up the edge slightly to form a rim. Spread with the tomato sauce, almost to the edge.

4 Arrange the meatballs on the pizza with the pimientos and bacon. Sprinkle over the cheese and drizzle with a little olive oil. Season with salt and pepper.

5 Bake the pizza in a preheated oven, at 400°F/200°C, for 18–20 minutes, or until the edge is crisp and a golden-brown color.

6 Serve immediately, garnished with chopped fresh parsley.

Creamy Ham & Cheese Pizza

This traditional pizza uses a pastry shell and béchamel sauce to make a type of savory tart. Grating the pastry gives it a lovely nutty texture.

NUTRITIONAL INFORMATION

Calories	628	Sugars	.........5g
Protein	........19g	Fat	..........47g
Carbohydrate	...35g	Saturates	......16g

🥧 20 mins   🕐 40 mins

SERVES 4

I N G R E D I E N T S

9 oz/250 g flaky pastry, well chilled

3 tbsp butter

1 red onion, chopped

1 garlic clove, chopped

1½ oz/40 g strong flour, plus extra for dusting

1¼ cups milk

1¾ oz/50 g Parmesan cheese, finely grated, plus extra for sprinkling

2 eggs, hard-cooked, cut into fourths

3½ oz/100 g Italian pork sausage, such as feline salami, cut into strips

salt and pepper

sprigs of fresh thyme, to garnish

1 Fold the pastry in half and grate it into 4 individual tart pans, measuring 4 inches/10 cm across. Using a floured fork, press the pastry flakes down so they are even, there are no holes, and the pastry comes up the sides of the pan.

2 Line the pastry shells with foil and bake blind in a preheated oven, at 425°F/220°C, for 10 minutes. Lower the heat to 400°F/200°C, remove the foil, and cook the pastry shells for 15 minutes, or until golden and set.

3 Heat the butter in a pan. Add the chopped onion and garlic and cook for 5–6 minutes, or until softened.

4 Add the flour, stirring well to coat the onions. Gradually stir in the milk to make a thick sauce.

5 Season the sauce with salt and pepper to taste and then stir in the Parmesan cheese. Do not reheat once the cheese has been added or the sauce will become too stringy.

6 Spread the sauce over the pastry shells. Decorate with the eggs and strips of sausage.

7 Sprinkle with a little extra Parmesan cheese, return to the oven, and bake for 5 minutes, just to heat through.

8 Serve immediately, garnished with sprigs of fresh thyme.

COOK'S TIP

These pizzas are just as good cold, but do not prepare them too far in advance because the pastry will turn soggy.

Corned Beef Hash Pizza

A combination of corned beef and baked eggs on a sour cream and potato base makes a really unusual pizza.

NUTRITIONAL INFORMATION

Calories .... 563 Sugars 16g
Protein .... 36g Fat 28g
Carbohydrate ... 45g Saturates 12g

1¼ hrs   35 mins

SERVES 4

INGREDIENTS

1 lb 2 oz/500 g potatoes, peeled

3 tbsp sour cream

1 tbsp olive oil, for greasing

11½ oz/325 g canned corned beef

1 small onion, finely chopped

1 green bell pepper, chopped

3 tbsp tomato and chile relish

1 quantity Special Tomato Sauce (see page 9)

4 eggs

1 oz/25 g mozzarella cheese, grated

1 oz/25 g colby cheese, grated

paprika

salt and pepper

chopped fresh parsley, to garnish

1 Cut the potatoes into even-size chunks. Boil in salted water for 5 minutes. Drain, rinse in cold water, and cool.

COOK'S TIP

For extra color, mix a grated carrot with the potato base. This will look and taste good, and will help persuade children to eat their vegetables, if they are fussy eaters. Use the tomato and chile relish sparingly if you are serving this to children.

2 Grate the potatoes and mix with the sour cream and seasoning in a bowl. Place on a large greased cookie sheet or pizza pan and pat out into a 10-inch/25-cm circle, pushing up the edge slightly to form a rim.

3 Mash the corned beef coarsely with a fork and stir in the onion, green bell pepper, and relish. Season well.

4 Spread the tomato sauce over the potato base almost to the edge. Top with the corned beef mixture. Using a spoon, make 4 wells in the corned beef. Carefully break an egg into each well.

5 Mix the cheeses together and sprinkle over the pizza with a little paprika. Season with salt and pepper.

6 Bake in a preheated oven, at 400°F/200°C, for 20-25 minutes, until the eggs have cooked but still have slightly runny yolks.

7 Serve immediately, garnished with chopped parsley.

Hot Chile Beef Pizza

This deep-pan pizza is topped with ground beef, red kidney beans, and jalapeño chiles, which are small, green, and very hot.

NUTRITIONAL INFORMATION

Calories ......550 Sugars 5g
Protein ....24g Fat 26g
Carbohydrate ...60g Saturates 9g

1½ hrs   30 mins

SERVES 4

I N G R E D I E N T S

DEEP-PAN DOUGH

¾ oz/20 g fresh yeast, or 1½ tsp dry or rapid-rise dry yeast

½ cup tepid water

1 tsp sugar

3 tbsp olive oil, plus extra for greasing

generous 1½ cups all-purpose flour, plus extra for dusting

1 tsp salt

TOPPING

1 small onion, thinly sliced

1 garlic clove, crushed

½ yellow bell pepper, chopped

1 tbsp olive oil

6 oz/175 g lean ground beef

¼ tsp chili powder

¼ tsp ground cumin

7 oz/200 g canned red kidney beans, drained

1 quantity Basic Tomato Sauce (see page 5)

1 oz/25 g jalapeño chiles, sliced

2¼ oz/60 g mozzarella, thinly sliced

2¼ oz/60 g sharp colby cheese or Monterey Jack, grated

olive oil, for drizzling

salt and pepper

fresh parsley, chopped, to garnish

1 For the deep-pan dough base, use the same method as the Bread Dough Base recipe (see page 6) but use the ingredients listed here.

2 Roll out or press the dough, using a rolling pin or your hands, into a 9-inch/23-cm circle on a lightly floured counter. Place on a large greased cookie sheet or pizza pan and push up the edge to form a small rim. Cover and leave to rise slightly for about 10 minutes.

3 To make the topping, cook the onion, garlic, and bell pepper gently in the oil for 5 minutes, until soft but not browned. Increase the heat slightly and add the beef, chili powder, and cumin. Cook for 5 minutes, stirring occasionally. Remove from the heat. Stir in the kidney beans. Season well.

4 Spread the tomato sauce over the dough, almost to the edge. Top with the meat mixture.

5 Top with the chiles, mozzarella, and grated cheese. Drizzle with a little olive oil and season to taste.

6 Bake the pizza in a preheated oven, at 400°F/200°C, for 18–20 minutes, or until the crust is golden. Serve immediately sprinkled with chopped parsley.

Eggplant & Lamb Pizza

An unusual, fragrant, spiced pizza topped with ground lamb and eggplant on a bread base.

NUTRITIONAL INFORMATION

Calories 430   Sugars 10g
Protein ....18g   Fat 22g
Carbohydrate ...44g   Saturates 7g

🍲 3 hrs   🕐 30 mins

SERVES 4

I N G R E D I E N T S

1 small eggplant, diced

1 quantity Bread Dough Base (see page 6)

1 tbsp flour, for dusting

1 small onion, thinly sliced

1 garlic clove, crushed

1 tsp cumin seeds

1 tbsp olive oil

6 oz/175 g ground lamb

1 oz/25 g canned pimientos, thinly sliced

2 tbsp chopped fresh cilantro

1 quantity Special Tomato Sauce (see page 9)

3¼ oz/90 g mozzarella, thinly sliced

olive oil, for greasing and drizzling

salt and pepper

1 Place the diced eggplant in a colander, sprinkle with salt, and let the bitter juices drain for about 20 minutes. Rinse thoroughly, then pat dry with paper towels.

2 Roll out or press the dough, using a rolling pin or your hands, into a 10-inch/25-cm circle on a lightly floured counter. Place on a large greased cookie sheet or pizza pan and push up the edge to form a rim.

3 Cover and leave to rise slightly for 10 minutes in a warm place.

4 Cook the onion, garlic, and cumin seeds gently in the olive oil for 3 minutes. Increase the heat slightly and add the lamb, eggplant, and pimientos. Cook for 5 minutes, stirring occasionally. Add the cilantro and season with salt and pepper to taste.

5 Spread the tomato sauce over the dough base, almost to the edge. Top with the lamb mixture.

6 Arrange the mozzarella slices on top. Drizzle over a little olive oil and adjust the seasoning.

7 Bake the pizza in a preheated oven, at 400°F/200°C, for 18–20 minutes, or until the crust is crisp and golden. Serve the pizza immediately.